How Chubby the Cat was Found!

A True Story

The incredible true story
of how a cat survived
four weeks during the coldest
month of the year. It's a story
of never giving up hope
of finding him.

By Karen Howe and Denise F. Brown
Illustrated by Denise F. Brown

"How Chubby the Cat was Found! A True Story"
ISBN-13: 978-0-9977485-1-2
ISBN-10: 0-9977485-1-6

www.raccoonstudios.com
Published by Raccoon Studios
692 Sagamore Avenue, Portsmouth, NH 03801

For more information about Chubby the Cat, visit:
www.chubbythecat.com

Dedicated to:

All lost animals,
animal rescue organizations,
and friends who helped
look for Chubby.

This book is about a cat named Chubby,
who lives in a small town
in New Hampshire.

In the winter, it gets really cold outside,
and there's usually deep snow
on the ground.

But, on sunny days,
Chubby likes to go out
and sit on the steps to take a nap
in the warm sun.

Karen is Chubby's owner.
When it snows, she shovels the sidewalk for him
to make a path to the shed.

Chubby can hide under the shed and stay warm
if it gets windy and cold.

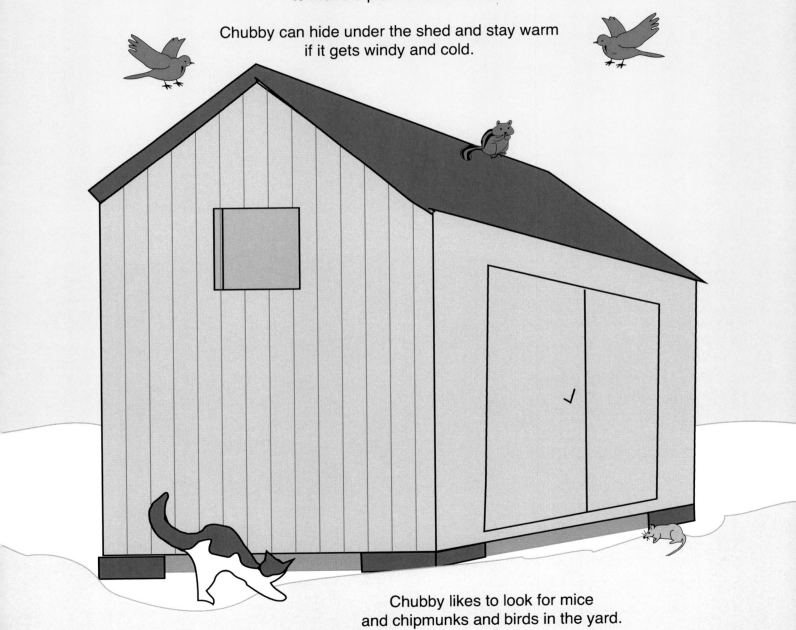

Chubby likes to look for mice
and chipmunks and birds in the yard.

After a nap, Chubby is always hungry!

CHUBBY

He knows Karen will feed him
as soon as she gets home from work.

When Chubby hears Karen's car
drive in the yard,
he races to the steps
to wait at the front door.

It's suppertime for Chubby!

Each day Karen says, "Hi, Chubby! How are you doing Chubby, baby!"
and opens the door
to let him in the house.

Chubby dashs to the kitchen.

First he gets a cat treat,
then Karen feeds him his favorite cat food — chicken with gravy!

"Chubby, you're so hungry!"
Karen says when she puts his plate on the floor.

After he licks up every bit of chicken,
Chubby walks into the living room
and stretchs out at his favorite spot on the floor
next to the big chair.

Now it's time to nap
and dream about all the mice and chipmunks
and birds outside.

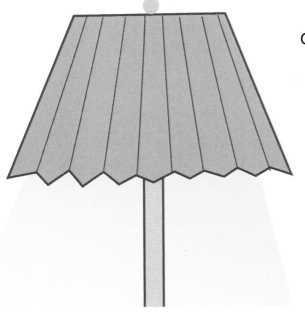

One night, Karen's husband, Sean, came home from work
and noticed Chubby was walking funny.
He picked the cat up and said,
"Let me take a look at your foot."

Sean told Karen, "The pads on his paw seem hurt.
Maybe you need to take Chubby to the vet?"

Karen said, "Okay, I'll take him tomorrow.
He needs his shots updated,
and maybe I'll get Chubby a new collar and i.d. tag."

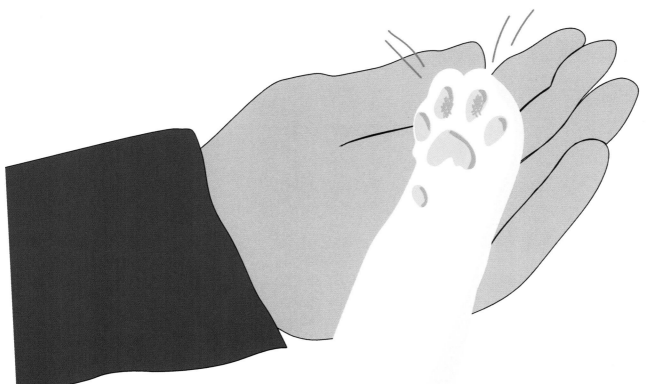

The next day Karen took Chubby to the vet,
but, at the veterinarian's parking lot,
a <u>terrible</u> thing happened.

Somehow, Chubby got out of his cat carrier
on the way to the vet.

Karen had to get out of the car to
reach for him in the back seat.

When she opened the car door just a tiny bit,
the cat saw his chance to escape!

He squeezed out of the car before Karen could catch him!

After Chubby jumped out of the car, he ran and hid under a green truck in the parking lot.

Karen didn't know what to do!

The road was a busy three-lane highway
with cars and trucks speeding by.

The truck driver didn't know Chubby was under his truck
and he started his engine!

When Chubby heard the engine start,
he jumped from under the green truck
and ran next door
to a junk yard full of wrecked cars.

Karen yelled, "Oh, no! Chubby!" and immediately
she ran through the snow after him.

Chubby slid on the ice and hid under the closest old car
he could get to.

Karen called and begged Chubby to come to her,
but he wouldn't come out
from under the old wrecked car.

He just 'meowed' back at her.

Karen knew Chubby was really scared.
She thought she should drive home
to get his cat treats and his blanket,
but, her house was five miles away!

Karen thought to herself,
"Will Chubby still be here when I get back?"

She had to do something, so she jumped in her car anyway
and drove home in a hurry.

"Meow"

"Meow"

Karen drove home as fast as she could.

She ran in the house
and grabbed Chubby's favorite treats and his blanket
and drove back to the parking lot,
but she wasn't <u>fast</u> enough.

Karen jumped out of her car and ran to look where she left Chubby.

He wasn't there!

She looked under every car in the parking lot,
calling for Chubby,
but the cat was nowhere to be found.

"Chubby!"

"Here,
Chubby!"

The worst part about losing Chubby was that it was early February
and freezing cold outside!

The parking lot and old cars were covered with ice and snow.

Karen looked all around her and under the cars.

Just behind the junk car lot were tall trees and woods
and a path leading to a snowmobile trail.

"Oh, no, wild animals live in those woods! I hope Chubby can hide from
the foxes and coyotes and bobcats who might be watching him."

"I have to find him, fast!"

Then Karen started to cry.
She didn't want to stop looking,
but it was getting dark out.

Finally, Karen had to go home without Chubby.

The next day, Karen went back to look for Chubby.

She posted "Missing Cat" flyers at the veterinarian's office and around town.

Karen went to the junk yard and searched under the cars
and near the snowmobile trail.
She called, "Here, Chubby! Come, Chubby!"

She looked around the houses and stores in the neighborhood,
but there was no trace of Chubby.

Karen needed help to search for Chubby,
so, she called her cousin, Denise, and told her that Chubby was lost.
"Denise, will you help me look for Chubby?"

Denise said, "Yes, of course I will!"

Together, Karen and Denise
walked past houses and
through the woods, calling for Chubby.
They searched along the snowmobile trail.
They followed cat tracks, dog tracks, raccoon tracks,
bobcat tracks, and deer tracks.

"Here, Chubby, Baby"

"Here, Kitty, Kitty!"

They walked for miles along nearby roads calling for Chubby.

They tried shaking cat food in a plastic cup
hoping Chubby would hear the familiar sound and come out of the woods,
or peek out from a stonewall.

They looked under sheds and barns,
and behind garages and warehouses.
They walked along frozen streams and looked under trees.

They looked any place a cat might hide
and take a nap.

They spoke to everyone they met along the way,
and asked,
"Have you seen a white and grey tiger cat?
His name is Chubby."

Sadly, no one had seen any lost or wandering cat that week.

One man they met said, "I have a digital wildlife camera on my shed,
but I only saw
a couple of raccoons and a fox."

Two weeks after Chubby went missing,
Denise read a town meeting notice on the town website.

She called Karen and said, "Maybe you should go to the meeting and
ask people if they saw Chubby. You can put up a 'Missing Cat' flyer at the Town Hall."

Karen rushed to the Town Hall and learned that
the meeting had been cancelled,
but a nice lady working in the office told her
she could put her "Missing Cat" flyer
on the town bulletin board.

Three weeks had gone by without finding Chubby.

A bad snowstorm was in the forecast for the next two days.
Karen was very worried about the blizzard that was coming and
she thought about the big trucks that would be plowing the snow.

Every morning before work, Karen drove around town, looking and calling for Chubby.
Karen thought to herself, "Oh, Chubby, I hope you're safe
and you've found something to eat and a place to sleep."

MISSING
CAT

Call
Sean or
Karen

Like   Comment   Share

Denise put "Missing Cat" posts
on social media sites
on her computer.

Many of her friends saw it and posted ideas
and positive thoughts and wishes
that Chubby would return home safely.

Now, *a month* had gone by since Chubby went missing.

The recent blizzard added a foot of snow on the ground
and the wind blew high snowdrifts along the roads.

Karen tried to sleep at night, but it was so cold and windy outside,
she couldn't stop worrying about her little cat, but she never gave up hope.

Each night Karen looked out the window for Chubby,
hoping and praying, "Maybe you'll find your way home soon, Chubby, baby."

She would tell herself, "Oh, Chubby, I know you're still alive!
You're a smart outdoor cat and
you know how to hunt and find shelter,"
trying not to cry.

One morning, Karen's cell phone rang, "Chirp! Chirp!"

Karen answered her phone,
and a lady named Robin exclaimed, "I think I have your cat!
I saw your flyer at the Town Hall
and it sure looks like your cat.
He's been living under my mobile home for the last few weeks.
He doesn't have a collar or i.d. tag, but he looks like the picture on the flyer!"

Robin told Karen, "We've been putting cat food out for him
on the top step each morning.
He jumps out of the hole under the trailer,
eats the cat food, and then
sits on the steps to warm up in the sun.

"chirp!
chirp!"

Karen couldn't *believe*
Chubby was found!

She told Robin, "I'll come over
as soon as I get out of work."

Karen called Denise
to meet her there. Denise said
she would drive right over to help!

Karen said, "Great, if you hold him,
I won't have to worry about him
getting away!"

Karen and Denise were on their way to pick up Chubby!

Robin's husband answered the door and stepped outside.
He told them, "I haven't seen the cat for a week,
but he might still be hiding under our mobile home."

Karen and Denise were so disappointed at what he said.
They thought Robin meant Chubby had been caught
and all they had to do was pick him up.

Robin's husband pointed to the hole in the fencing
that Chubby used to go under the mobile home.

Karen tried calling for Chubby, but no cat came out for her.

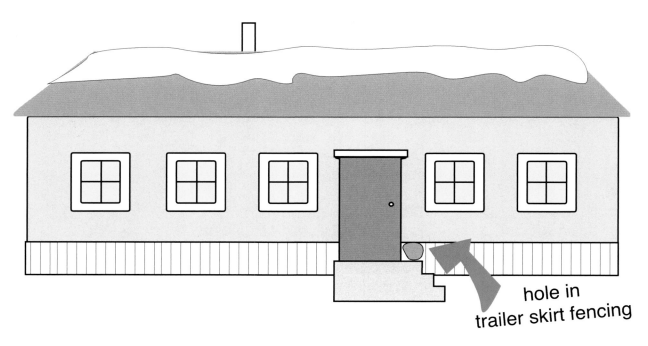

hole in
trailer skirt fencing

Denise said to Karen, "Let's look out back." They walked around the back
and noticed more openings that a cat could squeeze through.

"Maybe Chubby ran and hid in the woods,
or went to the house next door," said Karen.

Karen and Denise wondered what to do next
as they walked back to the car without Chubby.

They drove up the street and
knocked on doors of homes with the lights on,
but nobody had seen a cat outside.

It was getting late in the afternoon.
Instead of giving up for the day,
they went back to take one last look near the mobile home.

Karen stopped the car in the street and they looked
to see if a cat might be on the steps.

Then a police cruiser drove up behind Karen's car and flashed his blue lights.
The officer asked, "Is there anything wrong? Are you all right?"

Karen told him,"We're looking for my cat.
I put a flyer on the Police Station bulletin board a month ago."

"Oh, I saw your flyer," said the officer.
I'll let you know if I see a cat. Good luck!" and he drove off down the road.

Denise didn't want to leave yet, and said, "I don't think we should leave until we're absolutely sure he's not here. I brought a can of crabmeat with me. Let's try to lure Chubby out from under the trailer, if he's still hiding there."

They walked up to the steps and put some crabmeat in the bowl on the top step and went back to the car, and waited and watched for Chubby.

Karen exclaimed, "I think I see a cat looking through the hole!" Then Karen yelled, "Denise, there's a cat on the step! He looks like Chubby! *It's Chubby!*"

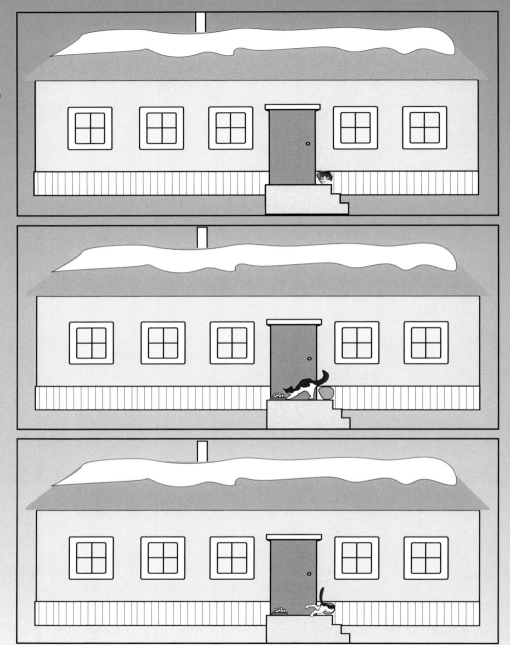

Karen and Denise got out of the car and slowly walked back up the icy driveway, but Chubby got scared and jumped back under the mobile home and stayed out of sight!

Karen and Denise didn't want to leave without Chubby, but it was dark and too cold to stay outside anymore. The temperature was almost zero degrees out.

They could see Chubby under the trailer watching them.
He smelled the crabmeat, but would not come out again.

Finally, Denise said, "I'm going to try to reach for him under the trailer."
She turned the flashlight toward Chubby.
All you could see were two big yellow, saucer-shaped eyes looking back.

Denise crawled under the trailer, but the cat backed up further and further
and hid behind some cardboard boxes, just out of reach of grabbing him.

Denise finally said, "Well, this is *not going to work*."
So, Karen and Denise decided they should leave him under the mobile home for the night.
"At least he's safe and warm."

The next day, Karen went back to the trailer
to try and coax Chubby out with cat treats.

Chubby seemed to recognize Karen, but he only stared back at her
and wouldn't come out.

"Why won't he come out for me?" Karen thought,
"Why is Chubby so afraid?"

Again, Karen went home without Chubby.

The next morning,
Robin's husband walked out the door
and onto the step at the exact same moment
Chubby jumped out from under the trailer!

He wasn't going to miss his chance to catch Chubby,
so he reached down and grabbed the cat and carried him into the house!

Robin was thrilled to call Karen and tell her,
"My husband caught your cat,
and he's safe inside our home."

Karen called the local cat rescue shelter to ask
if she could borrow a cat carrier.
They said, "Yes, and we'll drop it off at Robin's house."

The cat rescue lady arrived with the cat carrier and they quickly put Chubby into the cage.
She said, "Don't let him out of the carrier no matter what!"

Karen and Denise could hardly wait to go get Chubby!
When they walked into the trailer, there he was,
sitting quietly in the cat carrier, just staring out at them!

Chubby wasn't scared at all.

Robin's husband admitted to Karen,
"I gave the cat a rest from the cage and let him out in the bedroom this afternoon.
We took a nap together. He's such a good cat."

Karen thanked them
for taking such good care of Chubby.

Robin's husband asked to say goodbye to Chubby.
He opened the cage door a tiny bit and scratched the cat's chin
and said, "We really fell in love with this cat,
but we're glad he's going back to his home."

He closed the cat carrier door and carefully locked it.

Denise picked up the cat carrier and they walked to the car with Chubby,
trying not to slip on the ice and drop the cage.

Karen said, "I feel like I'm dreaming. Do we really have Chubby?"

Denise put the cat carrier on the front seat of the car on her lap
to make sure Chubby got home safely.
"This seems like I'm dreaming, too!" Denise said, "Chubby is really in your car!"

Karen backed out the driveway and drove to her house.

Chubby didn't even cry or meow.
He seemed to know where he was going.

When they got to Karen's home,
Denise carried the cat carrier into the kitchen
and Karen set Chubby free.

Chubby walked right up to his bowl,
ate his cat food, and used his litter box.

"Chubby, you're finally back home,
safe and sound!" said Karen,
"I'm so happy.
I can hardly believe you're here
in my kitchen."

Chubby licked his bowl clean
and walked to the living room,
and rubbed against the big comfy chair.

Chubby seemed relieved
to be back in his house.

He stretched out on his favorite spot
on the floor, as if to say
"Meow, I'm home now!"

He was back from his 'cat vacation' and acted like
nothing out of the ordinary had happened.
Everything was normal again!

Karen picked up Chubby and gave him a big hug,
and whispered in his ear,
"Chubby you're smarter than the average cat.
You found food and shelter for yourself for a month outside."

"I'm so thankful you're back home. I'll take care of you now."
The little cat seemed to purr louder than ever.

Chubby cuddled up to Karen and slept on her lap all night.

~ The End ~

How Chubby the Cat was Found

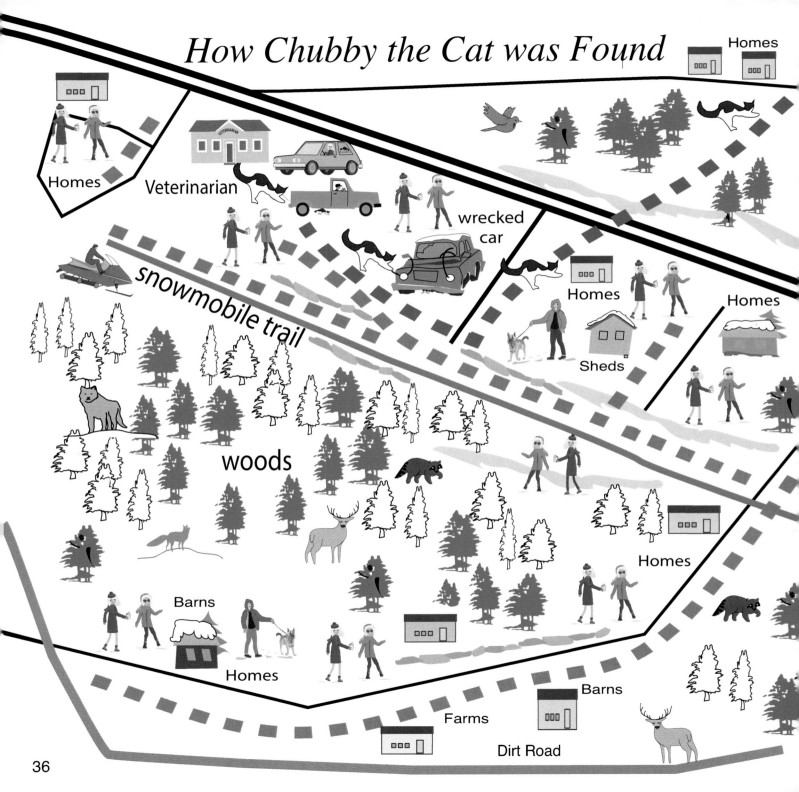

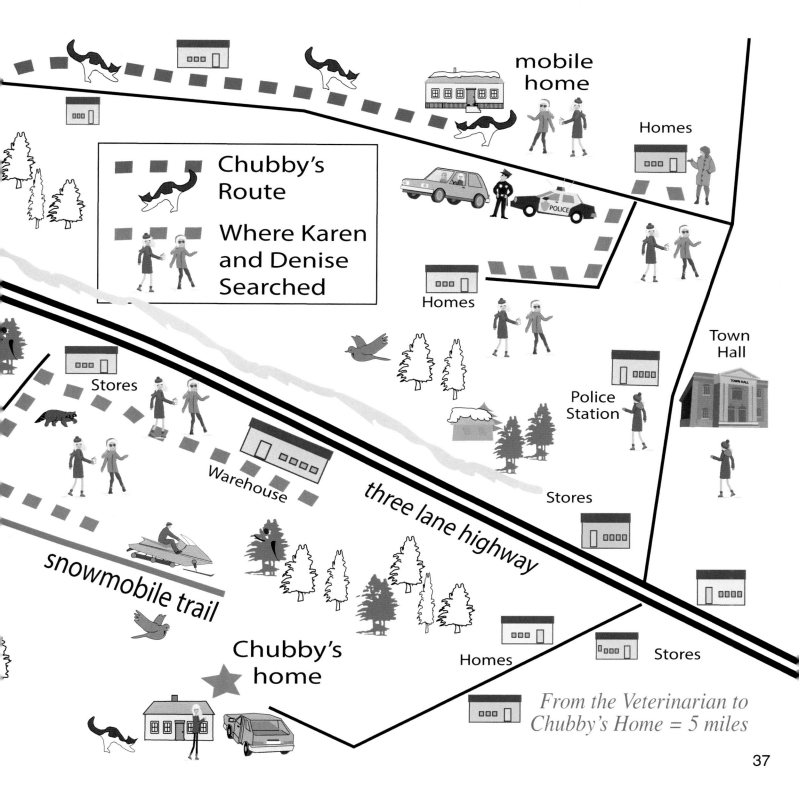

mobile home

Homes

Chubby's Route

Where Karen and Denise Searched

Town Hall

Homes

Police Station

Stores

Warehouse

three lane highway

snowmobile trail

Stores

Chubby's home

Homes

Stores

From the Veterinarian to Chubby's Home = 5 miles

About Chubby's owner,
Karen Howe

Karen Howe wanted to make a book about her cat named Chubby, an especially smart cat who is different from other cats. She asked her cousin Denise Brown, who is an artist and author, to collaborate together on this project. They started to work on the book about Chubby, writing and editing the story for several weeks.

Then one morning, Karen called Denise to tell her that Chubby was missing... That's when the whole story started over. They had to find Chubby and save him from the wild animals in the woods and the cold winter and snow. When he was finally found and brought back home, Karen and Denise knew they had to change the book to be about the search for Chubby and how he survived against the odds during the coldest month of the year.

Karen and Denise searched all the back roads and woods in the direction of Karen's home which was five miles away. They never thought Chubby would cross the busy three lane road, but at some point, he did. Then he walked almost two miles in the other direction from home where he found safety under a mobile home.

About the Co-Author and Illustrator,
Denise F. Brown

Denise F. Brown of Portsmouth, New Hampshire has authored, illustrated and produced many children's books for herself and for clients.

Denise is well known for her stunning watercolor paintings of Seacoast New England scenes, architectural renderings, horse illustrations, her pony figurine designs with The Trail of Painted Ponies, and childrens books.

She is the creator of her popular series of children's coloring books, *Ted Gets Out,* which celebrates the adventures of one of her cats.

Denise is the author and illustrator of *Wind: Wild Horse Rescue* adventure book, and children's books: *Abenaki, the Indian Pony* about a little horse who travels across the country, *A Deer Visits Nubble Lighthouse, a true story* about a young deer who is trapped on the island at high tide, and *USS Albacore Submarine*, about the famous little submarine built in Portsmouth, NH.

Denise illustrated and produced *Tugboat River Rescue, The Badcats of Biddeford* and *The Memorial Bridge Cat* by Crystal Ward Kent.

Brown, along with husband, John O'Sullivan, own Ad-Cetera Graphics and Raccoon Studios of Portsmouth.

See Denise's artwork and books at:

www.raccoonstudios.com
ww.tugboatrescue.com
www.windwildhorse.com
www.adceteragraphics.com

"Being an animal lover, the news of Chubby being lost was heart wrenching! For a month, we kept searching and hoping Chubby found food and shelter. It was wonderful to finally know he was safe and back to his home. I was glad to be part of Chubby's story, with its happy ending."
— Denise Brown

What to Do
When a Pet is Missing:

People love their cats, dogs and horses. They are like family members.

When a pet is missing, lost or stolen, the owner's world is turned upside down. A roller coaster of emotions takes over — you worry all day, and you can't sleep at night.

There is no guarantee that you will find your pet, but you need to make a plan and you need to begin immediately.

- Ask a friend to walk around your neighborhood with you to look for your pet. Bring treats or food. Call your pet and then wait a while to see if he comes out of a hiding place. Knock on doors and talk to people out for a walk or walking their dog, and ask if anyone has seen your pet.

- Post and handout flyers in all directions of where your pet was last seen within a 2-5 mile radius. Include photos of your pet and your phone number (that is hooked up to an answering machine.) Post a flyer at the police station, town hall, library, stores, animal shelters, restaurants, gas stations, pet stores, and the highway department.

- If your pet has been microchipped, go to the web page of the chip registry to update the microchip registry information — phone numbers, your veterinarian and your contact info. Have the registry 'flag' the registration noting your pet is lost or stolen.

- Call and go to the local animal shelters yourself, within 20 miles of your search, to look at the pets that have been brought in — at least every other day if possible.

  — The animal might be dirty or neglected looking so your description might not match what you tell them over the phone. Your pet might not be listed yet or may have lost their collar or tag.

  — Some shelters do not keep pets for more than a few days, or they try to adopt them out quickly, so you must keep checking often. Call animal control and the local police department, and ask if any pet has been picked up.

- Post your missing pet info online on social media and Missing Pet sites, and in local and surrounding area newspapers.

- The last resort is to check highway departments or shelters for deceased animals.

- Of most importance is to never give up hope. Many people are happy to help you find your pet.

Our Mission:

"How Chubby the Cat Was Found" is a true story about a lost cat named Chubby and how his owner never gave up hope of finding him and did everything possible to find him.

The story is an emotional adventure with an uplifting happy ending, and relates to all people who love animals, have owned animals, or have lost a pet.

It includes suggestions for what to do when a pet is lost or missing, and may help to save pets lives and reunite them with their families. That's why we want other people to read and share Chubby's story.

"We don't want anyone else to go through this if we can be of some help with this book."
— Karen Howe

Chubby back in his home

Chubby was adopted by Karen. He's a normal weight for an adult cat, but he was probably a lovable, roly poly kitten, hence the name, Chubby. Being outside for a month, he did lose a couple pounds. Karen is feeding him an extra meal now that he is home recovering from his cat adventure.

Made in the USA
Columbia, SC
21 September 2019